W9-BLX-285

Selected

Poems

In
Five
Sets

OTHER BOOKS BY LAURA (RIDING) JACKSON
PUBLISHED BY PERSEA

The Poems of Laura Riding: A New Edition of the 1938 Collection
First Awakenings: The Early Poems of Laura Riding
The Word "Woman" and Other Related Writings
Four Unposted Letters to Catherine

LAURA RIDING

Selected

Poems

In

Five

Sets

Selection and preface by Laura (Riding) Jackson

Persea Books
New York

First published in 1970 by Faber & Faber, Ltd.
First U.S. edition published in 1973;
republished by Persea Books in 1993.

Copyright © 1938 by Laura Riding
This edition copyright © 1970 by Laura (Riding) Jackson,
transferred in 1991 to The Board of Literary Management
of the late Laura (Riding) Jackson

All rights reserved. No part of this publication may be
reproduced or transmitted in any form or by any means,
electronic or mechanical, including photocopy, recording,
or any information storage and retrieval system without
prior permission in writing from the publisher.

Requests for permission to reprint or to make copies and
for any other information should be addressed
to the publisher:

Persea Books, Inc.
60 Madison Avenue
New York, New York 10010

Library of Congress Cataloging-in-Publication Data

Jackson, Laura (Riding), 1901–
[Poems. Selections]
Laura Riding : selected poems in five sets / selection and
preface by Laura (Riding) Jackson.
p.   cm.
ISBN 0-89255-189-5 : $9.95
I. Title.   II. Title: Selected poems.
PS3519.A363A6   1993
811'.52—dc20   92-38484
CIP

First paperback printing

To Patricia Butler

(my English agent) who, sure
friend to the end, and beyond,
forwarded this book with glad
feeling as she put her desk in
final order. And, Charles Mon-
teith, friend to the book in its
English publication (with others
of Faber & Faber).

And to Sonia Raiziss

(American writer, editor) who,
long devoted to my poems, was
the first in later time to write
feelingly on them. And, Michael
Kirkham (English critic), who,
after her, wrote courageously, on
them.

Contents

SET III

SET IV

SET V

Preface

MY history as one who was for long a devout advocate of poetry, and then devoutly renounced allegiance to it as a profession and faith in it as an institution, raises a question of consistency. Those who know my poems — those who have cared for them, those who have not, those who have drawn from their inner attitude and their linguistic qualities propulsive force for attempts to transcend (in their own poems) mere period-modernism — have for the most part (as the indications go) shrugged off my change of view of poetry as exhibiting an inconsistency so bizarre as to be explicable only in private-life terms. This notion has seemed justified by my protracted public silence on the subject. By 1962 I had made but a single statement on it in print, and that, coming before I had explored all the significances of the new view, was a cautious generalization. The impression that my break with poetry might not be a critically responsible act was strengthened by the infusion of colourable insinuations into the flow-ways of literary rumour.

When at last I began to speak explicitly on my changed view of poetry, the question of consistency was my first concern, but not in relation to myself as one who had lapsed from it extraordinarily, mysteriously. The story I had to tell was of my becoming so much aware of a discrepancy, deep-reaching, between what I call the creed and the craft of poetry — which I might otherwise describe as its religious and its ritualistic aspects — that I perceived the impossibility of anyone's functioning with consistency in the character of poet. Two exceptions to this impossibility must be made. There is a formal consistency possible in ever-prolonged evasion of the challenge to honor with which poetry confronts its practising devotees, and there is an organic consistency up to a point, the point in consistent endeavor to meet the challenge where awareness comes (as come it must, in such endeavour) of an ultimate impossibility of meeting it and remaining a poet.

I can make here only a meagre identification of the challenge poetry holds: what compatibility can there be between the creed offering hope of a way of speaking beyond the ordinary, touching perfection, a complex perfection associable with nothing less complex than truth, and the craft tying the hope to verbal rituals that court sensuosity as if it were the judge of truth? Straining of effort to achieve compatibility between these will lend moral coherence to the effort, and for long employ a native will in a poet to consistency. If poets strain hard enough they must reach the crisis-point at which division between creed and craft reveals itself to be absolute. If, with intuition of final trouble ahead, they slacken the straining to a slow, morally comfortable rate of subsidence, neither they nor their public will feel anything worse to be happening than a tempering of moral intensity to the dignity of advancing maturity. The backing-away of poets of better-than-average conscience from extreme testing of the possibilities of consistency in the poet-rôle passes unnoticed because no poet before me has gone to the very breaking-point: there is nothing in the poetic corpus to suggest the pertinence to poetry of a higher standard of scrupulosity than that observed in its historic best. Someone cited Rimbaud to me in this connection; but it was not in the cause of consistency that he abandoned the poet-rôle. (I shall speak of him again.)

I have distinguished a formal consistency as peculiar to certain poetic procedure. In this procedure there is also a straining of effort, but the challenge to honor is never answered in this straining: all effort is expended in problems of craft. Such straining can be highly intense, and simulate, in its intensity, straining of the kind aimed at keeping a moral proportion between poetic craft and the sacred poetic motive; and it can seem to be blessed with success because the results appear to be 'good' poems, the actual tinkering being concealed under carefully mixed and applied literary polish. Further, a sanctimony of seriousness about poetry always accompanies craft-straining, and, functioning as a guarantee of good quality, excites a predisposition to confidence: though the procedure does not rise above poetic journalism, the steady-handedness with which it is conducted has the noble appearance of moral care. The difference between such industry and the moral strenuosities of those who try to make one sense of the two senses of poetry has never been distinctly appreciated, and has become obscured in the thickening opacity of the problem of poetry as a problem in the field of language of extensive human importance.

The work of poets taken in period-mass is very difficult to order qualitatively for any one period without arbitrary critical differentiations. It probably presents more confusion, characteristically, than a period-mass of the work of other literary professionals, or of the professionals of other areas of 'culture'-activity, poetic performance being of its outspeaking nature more personalized and more subject, thus, to individual variation. I venture the observation, at any rate, as one able to contemplate the immediate poetic scene (against the background of antecedent poetic vistas) with the objectivity of a non-competitor and a critic having only general human, extramural, affiliations, that never before has there been so great a variety of individual poet-styles, and so much poverty of thematic content of the kind the word 'poetry', in the entire virtue of its meaning, signifies—religious (to use the word again) in magnitude of scope and purity of interest-value. The total display crackles with craft-individualism, but there is no sparkling, no brilliance: all is suffused with a light of drab poetic secularity.

Having shown some general aspects of the question of consistency, I take up again the tale of myself.

The last poems I wrote are contained in my *Collected Poems*, published in 1938. I can be seen, in that book, to be striving to find at once the poetic extreme and, in it, the mark of human fullness of utterance—and to be heading towards finalities of proof of poetry, and of the poet-rôle itself. There is also to be seen there a movement of developing sensibility, above the personal or professional, reflecting consciousness-at-large of the approach of human life in the whole to a term, and of there being, to come, *something after*. The

13

relation of the sense of a something-after to the striving is, precisely, that of religious sensibility giving itself into the keeping of poetic sensibility, which has a partial identity with it, but is, also, otherwise engaged. Poetry invites vision of a lasting, living fact awaiting our arrival at a state of grace in which we know it, *speak* it; it is also the patron of a historic love of the patterning of words with a physically ordered nicety, pleasing to human pride. I forced the issue, in my poems, of the spiritual serviceability of what has been regarded in all past human ages, and automatically continues so to be in this, as the universal type of the spiritual best in language.

In my preface to the collected edition of my poems, written with my commitment to poetry more ardent than ever, I spoke of poetry as being the actual process of realizing 'the good existence', described, itself, as 'poetry positive, all of truth': there was an ultimate of perfect truth to reach, and poetry was the way. Certainly, no other language-path had yet opened before this most comprehensive aspiration! When I had sealed the book with the preface, I had, I later knew, sealed my labors of poet. I felt at least, then, that the going-on would be different, would have a new decisiveness. I told my friends of the time that I foresaw a pause in poems-making of perhaps as much as four years. In less time than that I saw that I had reached poetry's limit.

The taint of complaisance stands out sharply in the backward look at poetry. Generally, in the composition of human customs, there is a self-complaisance that obliges aspiration to yield immediate satisfactions to pride. The craft-requisites of poetry accommodate the urgency, in it. I think of a terrible early poem of mine, 'The Mask', in which I stumbled into a clear vision of this actuality, though not a clear understanding of it. I include it in my selection with a prefatorial gloss: the 'taint' referred to in the poem is eternal only if poetry is eternal. But the course to the margin where this is knowable is hard, uncomfortable. I know of no one besides myself and my husband Schuyler (who, a poet, but, beyond that, a scholar of poetry, familiar as a brother with the yearning mansoul in it) who has put feet across the margin on the further ground — the margin being the knowledge that truth begins where poetry ends (or, as I said in introducing a BBC reading of my poems, that, for the practice of the style of truth to become a thing of the present, poetry must become a thing of the past). I have initiated enough poets into the idea of linguistic discipline for truth's sake, in the past, to know how verbally insensitive to considerations of truth poets can be, though behaving as persons born privy to it. In recent time, a few poets have professed agreement with my later view of poetry, and returned to their desks believing they could beat the impossibility that they had acknowledged. A word, now, as to Rimbaud's quitting poetry, and mine. In the poetic adventure, I had a structure of hope for shelter, whatever happened; and my inspiration came from everywhere. He was inspired by desperation; he flung it out, it narrowed fast back upon him, and would have destroyed him eventually had he not run away from it. For me, the essence of the adventure was in the words; he used them as stuff from which to distil an elixir giving power to make happiness out of unhappiness.

In a book on language by my husband and myself (long in the making, still a third short of completion when he died, July 4th, 1968), we speak of poetry, and make reference to my poetic work. 'Her objective in poetry may be said to have gone beyond the poetic as a literary category and reached into the field of the general human ideal in speaking . . . She tried to find in poetry the key to a way of speaking that would realize this spiritual ideal . . . looking to an eventual solution in poetry of the universal problem of how to make words fulfil the human being and the human being fulfil words.' Readers will, I hope, better understand my poems, and the sequel to them as well, for my stressing, here, the conflict in poetry between the motive of humanly perfect word-use and that of artistically perfect word-use — though I know how difficult it is for people to see the latter, which seems so much an innocent contributor of loveliness, as a parasitic partner in the poetic enterprise, taking an unholy share, ever over-large, in its management, and the honors. And just what is the sequel to my poems? I have written that which I believe breaks the spell of poetry; but I must be in no hurry as to that. I rest here

15

at saying that this preface is itself part of the sequel: I do not agree to the re-presentation of my poems unless (and for long there was no 'unless') I have leave to tell why there are no more — or an equivalent commentary is made on my behalf. With my poems and the commentary I point to the predicament in which poetry locks tongue, ear, the organs of feeling and intelligence, and even the sum of being, the soul; my poems are good illustrations of poetry, and as such may be considered to be also part of the sequel.

There will be reading of the poems in this book without reference to the preface, and with my consciousness of this goes an inconsistency in co-operating in making them available, since it is not my interest merely to add to the quantity of easily available poetic reading-matter. I judge my poems to be things of the first water as poetry, but that does not make them better than poetry, and I think poetry obstructs general attainment to something better in our linguistic way-of-life than we have. I can only hope that the poems themselves will soften this inconsistency by making the nature of poetry, to which they are faithful, plainer, in its forced, fine, suspension of truth; poetry and truth have both been so much hashed that there is little whole perception of what they are.

To many the poems will be new. Yet my poetic work has not been entirely forgotten in the period of its suppression by me. Indeed, it has served — both before and during this and continuously — as a new primer of poetic linguistics for many poets, and has been a source, more and more unidentified, of new poetic sophistication, generally (the gist of it all, however, being left to itself). A critical routine in my regard is to ascribe influence to me on certain ones, and fix it as terminating with the thirties, so much having been ingested, differently in each case, that as influence it is most conveniently treated as having disappeared. Criticism of my poetic work has on the whole been shy, with exceptions both beautiful and ugly, and tending towards irrelevancy (the queerest recent example being a suggestion in a poetry reference-book of relationship to Jean Wahl, and Nietzsche!). But I am not concerned with getting critical justice done to my poems: they were never my cause, though poetry once was. My cause is something poetry fails to be — belying its promissory advertisement of itself. May the poems of this selection excite some sense of wherein the failure of poetry lies, and some fore-sense of what that something might be.

I have arranged the selected poems in part by a rule of temporality, in part with an eye to reproducing the natural emphases and unities of my poetic work in its total character as a progression — placing some later poems with earlier ones, moving some earlier ones (though fewer and fewer, progressively) variously forward, according to the general course of insistencies in the work. That there are no sharp differences of trend between the 'sets' of poems, only differences in the balance-point of each, is not by contrivance, but reflects the fact that, though the weight of what I put into my poetic scales mounted as I went on, the scales were the same ones throughout, from the beginning.

Of myself, I should not omit a great deal from my *Collected Poems*, from which these poems are selected to make a handy reprint: so much curtailment of the story that the *Poems* tells makes all go too fast; likewise, a proportionate reduction of what I now have to say prefatorially on my poems overlightens the burden, the sense. But this book has had a happier history than suggested larger reproductions of my poetic work — I give it my blessing unreservedly.

I have departed from the text of my *Collected Poems* only for the correction of a few misprints, and a few small verbal changes, in which, mainly, I have reverted to earlier textual forms.

LAURA (RIDING) JACKSON

Wabasso, Florida

The Troubles of a Book

The trouble of a book is first to be
No thoughts to nobody,
Then to lie as long unwritten
As it will lie unread,
Then to build word for word an author
And occupy his head
Until the head declares vacancy
To make full publication
Of running empty.

The trouble of a book is secondly
To keep awake and ready
And listening like an innkeeper,
Wishing, not wishing for a guest,
Torn between hope of no rest
And hope of rest.
Uncertainly the pages doze
And blink open to passing fingers
With landlord smile, then close.

The trouble of a book is thirdly
To speak its sermon, then look the other way,
Arouse commotion in the margin,
Where tongue meets the eye,
But claim no experience of panic,
No complicity in the outcry.
The ordeal of a book is to give no hint
Of ordeal, to be flat and witless
Of the upright sense of print.

The trouble of a book is chiefly
To be nothing but book outwardly;
To wear binding like binding,

Bury itself in book-death,
Yet to feel all but book;
To breathe live words, yet with the breath
Of letters; to address liveliness
In reading eyes, be answered with
Letters and bookishness.

Postponement of Self

I took another day,
I moved to another city,
I opened a new door to me.
Then again a last night came.
My bed said: 'To sleep and back again?'
I said: 'This time go forward.'

Arriving, arriving, not yet, not yet,
Yet yet arriving, till I am met.
For what would be her disappointment
Coming late ('She did not wait').
I wait. And meet my mother.
Such is accident.
She smiles: long afterwards.
I sulk: long before.
I grow to six.
At six little girls in love with fathers.
He lifts me up.
See. Is this Me?
Is this Me I think
In all the different ways till twenty.
At twenty I say She.
Her face is like a flower.
In a city we have no flower-names, forgive me.
But flower-names not necessary
To diary of identity.

The Rugged Black of Anger

The rugged black of anger
Has an uncertain smile-border.
The transition from one kind to another
May be love between neighbour and neighbour;
Or natural death; or discontinuance
Because, so small is space,
The extent of kind must be expressed otherwise;
Or loss of kind when proof of no uniqueness
Confutes the broadening edge and discourages.

Therefore and therefore all things have experience
Of ending and of meeting,
And of ending that much more
As self grows faint of self dissolving
When more is the intenser self
That is another too, or nothing.
And therefore smiles come of least smiling —
The gift of nature to necessity
When relenting grows involuntary.

This is the account of peace,
Why the rugged black of anger
Has an uncertain smile-border,
Why crashing glass does not announce
The monstrous petal-advance of flowers,
Why singleness of heart endures
The mind coupled with other creatures.
Room for no more than love in such dim passages
Where between kinds lie only
Their own uncertain edges.

This such precise division of space
Leaves nothing for walls, nothing but
Weakening of place, gentleness.
The blacker anger, blacker the less
As anger greater, angrier grows;

And least where most,
Where anger and anger meet as two
And share one smile-border
To remain so.

Incarnations

Do not deny,
Do not deny, thing out of thing.
Do not deny in the new vanity
The old, original dust.

From what grave, what past of flesh and bone
Dreaming, dreaming I lie
Under the fortunate curse,
Bewitched, alive, forgetting the first stuff . . .
Death does not give a moment to remember in

Lest, like a statue's too transmuted stone,
I grain by grain recall the original dust
And, looking down a stair of memory, keep saying:
This was never I.

The Why of the Wind

We have often considered the wind,
The changing whys of the wind.
Of other weather we do not so wonder.
These are changes we know.
Our own health is not otherwise.
We wake up with a shiver,
Go to bed with a fever:
These are the turns by which nature persists,
By which, whether ailing or well,

We variably live,
Such mixed we, and such variable world.
It is the very rule of thriving
To be thus one day, and thus the next.
We do not wonder.
When the cold comes we shut the window.
That is winter, and we understand.
Does our own blood not do the same,
Now freeze, now flame within us,
According to the rhythmic-fickle climates
Of our lives with ourselves?

But when the wind springs like a toothless hound
And we are not even savaged,
Only as if upbraided for we know not what
And cannot answer —
What is there to do, if not to understand?
And this we cannot,
Though when the wind is loose
Our minds go gasping wind-infected
To our mother hearts,
Seeking in whys of blood
The logic of this massacre of thought.

When the wind runs we run with it.
We cannot understand because we are not
When the wind takes our minds.
These are lapses like a hate of earth.
We stand as nowhere,
Blow from discontinuance to discontinuance,
Then flee to what we are
And accuse our sober nature
Of wild desertion of itself,
And ask the reason as a traitor might
Beg from the king a why of treason.

We must learn better
What we are and are not.

We are not the wind.
We are not every vagrant mood that tempts
Our minds to giddy homelessness.
We must distinguish better
Between ourselves and strangers.
There is much that we are not.
There is much that is not.
There is much that we have not to be.
We surrender to the enormous wind
Against our learned littleness,
But keep returning wailing
'Why did I do this?'

From *Memories of Mortalities*
My Father and my Childhood

As childhood is to fairies, fancies,
Briefness of thought, and of heart
Fast change from hot to cool —
A flickering purpose, wild, then weak,
First passion, then a fear and pouting
On clumsy fingers told, and spent
In clumsy shadows, petulances
Spread in swollen tear-mist:
By such uncertain tides
I lived those doubtful years a child —
When to be live was half-felt sting
Of destiny, and half-stirred sleep of chance.
That was the time of tales —
Rising of mind to fragmentary hours
And fleshward fall by night
To scarce roused sloth of self.

For which I took a fox to father.
From many grinning tales he came
Sorrowed to that lonely burrow

Where the snake my mother left me
Cruelly to find what world I might
To history in, to get my name of.
There came the fox my father,
Between the tales to ponder, speak
The gruff philosophies of foxes:
'All is mistrust and mischief,
Bestiality and bestial comfort.
Life is a threadbare fiction —
Large the holes and thin the patches.
The gainer is the loser;
For to gain is to gain wisdom,
And wisdom's riches are the monies
In which poverty is counted —
To know how poor, how less than full
The gaping treasuries of truth,
Where's lack, what's niggard, which the fattened lie.'
Oh, famished fox-wit —
Hunger stanched with taste of hunger,
Shammed meals and cunning feints
And wily shifts to make one morrow more
Of failing fortune, duplication
Sour of sweets remembered sour.

Forth we went, this paternality
In careworn foxhood scrupulous
To teach the public pomp and private woes
Of social nature, crossed estate
Where reason's loud with nonsense
And nonsense soft with truth —
And I, droll pertinacity
To turn the random child-head round
In sphering wonder-habit
And step new-footed fervour
On whatever ground like books lay
To my learning docile, garrulous,
A world of self-blind pages,
Staring to be read.

Whether the misery more those tales
Through town and village scampering
With beggar-cry, to operatic heavens
From hoarse house-tops venting
Weather-vane conclusions, jangled morals,
Spasmed glees and glooms and thunders —
Or that from town to village countrywide
Homeless we stalked the straggling world,
Pursuing laws of change and sameness
To their momentary finish in
Equivocation's false repose —
Whether the plight more ours,
My father's, in his fox-despair
Driving that unlaughed laughter to hard grief,
A bigot brooding, fortitude
Of losses and mishoping,
And mine, in restive after-hope
Protracting death's impulsion of mere death
Till might be death-exceeding courage,
Perchance a love or loves to overreach
Time's mete of forwardness
And break with me the life-fast —
Or whether theirs more sorry burden,
That they built to heights and stretches
Direly not sufficing to be that
They climbed to, walked on, boasted
Sight-substantial, likely, thinkable,
Were countered in their caution
By stumblings, crumblings, mysteries
And mishaps disaccording
With their miserly assurance —

We did not make division
Between the world's calamitous revolving
And our sore travel with it
On roads toward starved renewal curved.
One bounden omen then the whole,
Community of presages

26

Not yet in strict dissemblance parted:
My mother's tears afall like leaves
The wind takes, not the earth,
Being upon the branch already dust;
My father's dour world-worrying,
The fabled fox into humaneness come
With stealthy nose and cynic tread
But smile less proud than anciently
When Time was less the common theme
And more the learned axiom;
The world's tossed mind, a ghost-sea
In dying deluge breaking
On all the secret shores of thought
Risen against Time's drowned horizon;
And I my living variance
From livingness, of death-kind
Live protagonist, whose mouth's 'to-day'
With morrows folded in from morrows
Hung speechlessly enwrapped.

And was it childhood, then,
From snake to fox's patronage,
And tortured idling, twisted course
Between the hither-thither stagger
Of the universal doom-day?
But was not childhood ever thus?
A premonition trembling distant
On lips of language shy,
Fast futures there acrowd
And quieted with story-book retard —
Even as I those troubled times of father
To story took and, parrying conclusion,
My fair curls shadowed among tales,
Made Imminence a dream-hush
Whose vocal waking slept inside my own.

There is no Land Yet

The long sea, how short-lasting,
From water-thought to water-thought
So quick to feel surprise and shame.
Where moments are not time
But time is moments.
Such neither yes nor no,
Such only love, to have to-morrow
By certain failure of now and now.

On water lying strong ships and men
In weakness skilled reach elsewhere:
No prouder places from home in bed
The mightiest sleeper can know.
So faith took ship upon the sailor's earth
To seek absurdities in heaven's name —
Discovery but a fountain without source,
Legend of mist and lost patience.

The body swimming in itself
Is dissolution's darling.
With dripping mouth it speaks a truth
That cannot lie, in words not born yet
Out of first immortality,
All-wise impermanence.

And the dusty eye whose accuracies
Turn watery in the mind
Where waves of probability
Write vision in a tidal hand
That time alone can read.

And the dry land not yet,
Lonely and absolute salvation —
Boasting of constancy
Like an island with no water round
In water where no land is.

From *Echoes*

Since learning all in such a tremble last night —
Not with my eyes adroit in the dark,
But with my fingers hard with fright,
Astretch to touch a phantom, closing on myself —
I have been smiling.

*   *   *

It was the beginning of time
When self hood first stood up in the slime.
It was the beginning of pain
When an angel spoke and was quiet again.

*   *   *

If there are heroes anywhere
Unarm them quickly and give them
Medals and fine burials
And history to look back on
As weathermen point with pride to rain.

*   *   *

Intelligence in ladies and gentlemen
And their children
Draws a broad square of knowledge
With their house walls.
But four corners to contain a square
Yield to an utmost circle —
The garden of the perpendicular is a sphere.

*   *   *

'I shall mend it,' I say,
Whenever something breaks,
'By tying the beginning to the end.'
Then with my hands washed clean
And fingers piano-playing
And arms bare to go elbow-in,
I come to an empty table always.
The broken pieces do not wait

29

On rolling up of sleeves.
I come in late always
Saying, 'I shall mend it.'

* * *

Gently down the incline of the mind
Speeds the flower, the leaf, the time —
All but the fierce name of the plant,
Imperishable matronymic of a species.

* * *

The poppy edifices of sleep,
The monotonous musings of night-breath,
The liquid featureless interior faces,
The shallow terrors, waking never far.

* * *

Love at a sickbed is a long way
And an untastable thing.
It hangs like a sickroom picture
And wears like another's ring.
Then the guarded yawn of pain snaps,
The immeasurable areas of distress
. . . . . . collapse . . .

* * *

. . . cheated history —
Which stealing now has only then
And stealing us has only them.

* * *

'Worthy of a jewel,' they say of beauty,
Uncertain what is beauty
And what the precious thing.

* * *

When a dog lying on the flagstones
Gazes into the sea of spring,
The surface of instruction
Does not ripple once:
He watches it too well.

* * *

Love is very everything, like fire:
Many things burning,
But only one combustion.

* * *

Let us seem to speak
Or they will think us dead, revive us.
Nod brightly, Hour.
Rescue us from rescue.

* * *

What a tattle-tattle we.
And what a rattle-rattle me.
What a rattle-tattle-tattle-rattle we-me.
What a rattle-tattle.
What a tattle-rattle.
What a we.
What a me.
What a what a
What a
What

SET II

The Nightmare

Of the two flowers growing
Each one side of the wall,
Which would the hungry child
In her nightmare
Pick to wear
If she did not fall
Frightened from the wall?

One was real,
One was false.
Both were same.

31

While she wavered they withered.
They died.
Hunger went.
There is no more a wall.
The nightmare is morning.
The child says, over-remembering:
Mother, the strangest thing,
Two flowers asleep,
One flower I saw, one I didn't,
One was alive, one was dead.
I was so hungry to be hungry.
Now I'll never know this way or that way,
Just because of breakfast and being awake.

The Mask

Cover up,
Oh, quickly cover up
All the new spotted places,
All the unbeautifuls,
The insufficiently beloved.

With what? with what?
With the uncovering of the lovelies,
With the patches that transformed
The more previous corruptions.

Is there no pure then?
The eternal taint wears beauty like a mask.
But a mask eternal.

Dear Possible

Dear possible, and if you drown,
Nothing is lost, unless my empty hands
Claim the conjectured corpse
Of empty water — a legal vengeance
On my own earnestness.

Dear creature of event, and if I wait the clock,
And if the clock be punctual and you late,
Rail against me, my time, my clock,
And rightfully correct me
With wrong, lateness and ill-temper.

Dear scholar of love,
If by your own formula
I open heaven to you
When you knock punctually at the door,
Then you are there, but I where I was.

And I mean that fate in the scales
Is up, down, even, trembling,
Right, wrong, weighing and unweighing,
And I mean that, dear possible,
That fate, that dear fate.

An Ageless Brow

This resolve: with trouble's brow
To forswear trouble and keep
A surface innocence and sleep
To smooth the mirror
With never, never,
And now, now.

The image, not yet in recognition, had grace
To be lasting in death's time, to postpone the face
Until the face had gone.
Her regiments sprang up here and fell of peace,
Her banners dropped like birds that had never flown.

And her arrested hand, clasping its open palm,
Pressed on from finger to finger
The stroke withheld from trouble
Till it be only ageless brow,
A renunciatory double
Of itself, a resolve of calm,
Of never, never, and now, now.

As Many Questions as Answers

What is to start?
It is to have feet to start with.
What is to end?
It is to have nothing to start again with,
And not to wish.

What is to see?
It is to know in part.
What is to speak?
It is to add part to part
And make a whole
Of much or little.
What is to whisper?
It is to make soft
The greed of speaking faster
Than is substance for.
What is to cry out?
It is to make gigantic
Where speaking cannot last long.

What is to be?
It is to bear a name.
What is to die?
It is to be name only.
And what is to be born?
It is to choose the enemy self
To learn impossibility from.
And what is to have hope?
Is it to choose a god weaker than self,
And pray for compliments?

What is to ask?
It is to find an answer.
What is to answer?
Is it to find a question?

Lucrece and Nara

Astonished stood Lucrece and Nara,
Face flat to face, one sense and smoothness.
'Love, is this face or flesh,
Love, is this you?'
One breath drew the dear lips close
And whispered,
'Nara, is there a miracle can last?'
'Lucrece, is there a simple thing can stay?'

Unnoticed as a single raindrop
Broke each dawn until
Blindness as the same day fell.
'How is the opalescence of my white hand, Nara?
Is it still pearly-cool?'
'How is the faintness of my neck, Lucrece?
Is it blood shy with warmth, as always?'

Ghostly they clung and questioned
A thousand years, not yet eternal,
True to their fading,

Through their long watch defying
Time to make them whole, to part them.
A gentle clasp and fragrance played and hung
A thousand years and more
Around earth closely.
'Earth will be long enough,
Love has no elsewhere.'

And when earth ended, was devoured
One shivering midsummer
At the dissolving border,
A sound of light was felt.
'Nara, is it you, the dark?'
'Lucrece, is it you, the quiet?'

One Self

Under apparel, apparel lies
The recurring body:
O multiple innocence, O fleshfold dress.

One self, one manyness,
Is first confusion, then simplicity.
Smile, death, O simultaneous mouth.
Cease, inner and outer,
Continuous flight and overtaking.

From *In Nineteen Twenty-Seven*

In nineteen twenty-seven, in the spring
And opening summer, dull imagination
Stretched the dollish smile of people.
Behind plate-glass the slant deceptive
Of footwear and bright foreign affairs
Dispelled from consciousness those bunions
By which feet limp and nations farce —

O crippled government of leather —
And for a season (night-flies dust the evening)
Deformed necessity had a greening.

Then, where was I, of this time and my own
A double ripeness and perplexity?
Fresh year of time, desire,
Late year of my age, renunciation —
Ill-mated pair, debating if the window
Is worth leaping out of, and by which.

*　　*　　*

The calendar and clock have stopped,
But does the year run down in time?
While time goes round? Giddying
With new renewal at each turning?

Thus sooner than it knows narrows
A year a year a year to another.
The season loses count, speeds on.
But I, charmed body of myself,
Am struck with certainty, stop in the street,
Cry 'Now' — and in despair seize love,
A short despair, soon over.
For by now all is history.

*　　*　　*

Fierce is unhappiness, a living god
Of impeccable cleanliness and costume.
In his intense name I wear
A brighter colour for the year
And with sharp step I praise him
That unteaches ecstasy and fear.
If I am found eating, loving,
Pleasure-making with the citizens,
These are the vigours learned of newspapers:
By such formalities I inhale
The corrupt oxygen of time

And reconstruct a past in which to wait
While the false curve of motion twitches straight.

*   *   *

Had I remained hidden and unmoved,
Who would have carried on this conversation
And at the close remembered the required toast
To the new year and the new deaths?
Oh, let me be choked ceremoniously
With breath and language, if I will,
And make a seemly world of it,
And live, if I will, fingering my fingers
And throwing yesterday in the basket.
I am beset with reasonableness,
Swallow much that I know to be grass,
Tip as earth tips and not from dizziness.
But do not call me false.
What, must I turn shrew
Because I know what I know,
Wipe out the riverfront
Because it stinks of water?
I cannot do what there is not to do.
And what there is to do
Let me do somewhat crookedly,
Lest I speak too plain and everlasting
For a weather-vane of understanding.

*   *   *

Therefore, since all is well,
Come you no nearer than the barrel-organ
That I curse off to the next square
And there love, when I hear it not.
For I have a short, kind temper
And would spare while I can.
While the season fades and lasts
I would be old-fashioned with it.
I would be persuaded it is so,
Go mad to see it run, as it were horses,

Then be unmaddened, find it done,
Summon you close, a memory long gone.

So I am human, of much that is no more
Or never was, and in a moment
(I must hurry) it will be nineteen twenty-eight,
An old eternity pleading a new year's grace.

Afternoon

The fever of afternoon
Is called afternoon,
Old sleep uptorn,
Not yet time for night-time,
No other name, for no names
In the afternoon but afternoon.

Love tries to speak but sounds
So close in its own ear.
The clock-ticks hear
The clock-ticks ticking back.
The fever fills where throats show,
But nothing in these horrors moves to swallow
While thirst trails afternoon
To husky sunset.

Evening appears with mouths
When afternoon can talk.
Supper and bed open and close
And love makes thinking dark.
More afternoons divide the night,
New sleep uptorn,
Wakeful suspension between dream and dream —
We never knew how long.
The sun is late by hours of soon and soon —
Then comes the quick fever, called day.
But the slow fever is called afternoon.

From *The Talking World*

Meeting on the way to the same there,
The tired ones talk and make a here,
And further is then where, and where?

*　　*　　*

Of such mixed intent
Places in time spring up,
And truth is anybody's argument
Who can use words untruthfully enough
To build eternity inside his own short mouth.

*　　*　　*

Great manyness there is
Before all becomes an all.
Uncertainty and criticism
Oppose to the unified eventual
A world of disagreement
In which every contradictory opinion
Is for to-day an 'I' wearing a crown
Of weeds plucked from the tip of the tongue.

*　　*　　*

And talk in talk like time in time vanishes.
Ringing changes on dumb supposition,
Conversation succeeds conversation,
Until there's nothing left to talk about
Except truth, the perennial monologue,
And no talker to dispute it but itself.

*　　*　　*

Let there be talk and let there be no talk.
Let the birds with the birds chirp of birds that chirp.
Let the wearers of coats with the wearers of coats
Speak the wisdom of coats, and with the coatmakers.
Let the uses of words prevail over words.

40

Let there be many ways of not lying
And no ways of truth-telling.
Let there be no wrong because no right.

*　　*　　*

And more of talk I cannot talk,
Except I talk, speak mingled.
And you would then attend,
Nor complain that I speak solitary.
But complain no more.
Look, I am gone from you,
From your immunity to death and listening.
May you for ever not know nor weather cease
Wherein to die in your own colours,
With other banners flying than the black.
May you not lose the sun too soon —
Blindness and noise by which you stand
Between yourselves and yourselves.
May you not know how never more you were
Than such and such mistalking,
O talking world that says and forgets.

By Crude Rotation

By crude rotation —
It might be as a water-wheel
Is stumbled and the blindfolded ox
Makes forward freshly with each step
Upon the close habitual path —
To my lot fell a blindness
That was but a blindedness,
And then an inexpressive heart,
And next a want I did not know of what
Through blindedness and inexpressiveness
Of heart.

To my lot fell
By trust, false signs, fresh starts,
A slow speed and a heavy reason,
A visibility of blindedness — these thoughts —
And then content, the language of the mind
That knows no way to stop.

Thus turning, the tragedy of self hood
And self-haunting smooths with turning,
While the worn track records
Another, and one more.

To my lot fell
Such waste and profit,
By crude rotation
Too little, too much,
Vain repetition,
The picture over-like,
Illusion of well-being,
Base lust and tenderness of self.

Fall down, poor beast,
Of poor content.
Fly, wheel, be singular
That in the name of nature
This creaking round spins out.

Mortal

There is a man of me that sows.
There is a woman of me that reaps.
One for good,
And one for fair,
And they cannot find me anywhere.

Father and Mother, shadowy ancestry,
Can you make no more than this of me?

The Wind Suffers

The wind suffers of blowing,
The sea suffers of water,
And fire suffers of burning,
And I of a living name.

As stone suffers of stoniness,
As light of its shiningness,
As birds of their wingedness,
So I of my whoness.

And what the cure of all this?
What the not and not suffering?
What the better and later of this?
What the more me of me?

How for the pain-world to be
More world and no pain?
How for the old rain to fall
More wet and more dry?

How for the wilful blood to run
More salt-red and sweet-white?
And how for me in my actualness
To more shriek and more smile?

By no other miracles,
By the same knowing poison,
By an improved anguish,
By my further dying.

Earth

Have no wide fears for Earth:
Its universal name is 'Nowhere'.
If it is Earth to you, that is your secret.
The outer records leave off there,
And you may write it as it seems,
And as it seems, it is,
A seeming stillness
Amidst seeming speed.

Heavens unseen, or only seen,
Dark or bright space, unearthly space,
Is a time before Earth was
From which you inward move
Toward perfect now.

Almost the place it is not yet,
Potential here of everywhere —
Have no wide fears for it:
Its destiny is simple,
To be further what it will be.

Earth is your heart
Which has become your mind
But still beats ignorance
Of all it knows —
As miles deny the compact present
Whose self-mistrusting past they are.
Have no wide fears for Earth:
Destruction only on wide fears shall fall.

Sleep Contravened

An hour was taken
To make the day an hour longer.
The longer day increased
In what had been unfinished.
Another hour from sleep was taken,
Till all sleep was contravened,
Yet the day's course
More long and more undone.

And the sleep gone.
And the same day goes on and on,
A mighty day, with sleeplessness
A gradual evening toward soon lying down.

Soon, soon.
And sleep forgotten,
Like: What was birth?
And no death yet, the end so slowly,
We seem departing but we stay.

And if we stay
There will be more to do
And never through though much is through.
For much keeps the eyes so much open,
So much open is so much sleep forgotten,
Sleep forgotten is sleep contravened,
Sleep contravened is so much longer mind,
More thought, more speaking,
Instead of sleep, blinking, blinking,
Blinking upright and with dreams
Same as all usual things,
Usual things same as all dreams.

The Quids

The little quids, the monstrous quids,
The everywhere, everything, always quids,
The atoms of the Monoton,
Each turned an essence where it stood,
Ground a gisty dust from its neighbours' edges,
Until a powdery thoughtfall stormed in and out —
The cerebration of a slippery quid enterprise.

Each quid stirred.
The united quids
Waved through a sinuous decision.
The quids, that had never done anything before
But be, be, be, be, be —
The quids resolved to predicate,
To dissipate themselves in grammar.

Oh, the Monoton didn't care,
For whatever they did —
The Monoton's contributing quids —
The Monoton would always remain the same.

A quid here and there gyrated in place-position,
While many turned inside-out for the fun of it.
And a few refused to be anything but
Simple unpredicated copulatives.
Little by little, this commotion of quids,
By ones, by tens, by casual millions,
Squirming within the state of things,
The metaphysical acrobats,
The naked, immaterial quids,
Turned in on themselves
And came out all dressed —
Each similar quid of the inward same,
Each similar quid dressed in a different way,
The quids' idea of a holiday.

The quids could never tell what was happening.
But the Monoton felt itself differently the same
In its different parts.
The silly quids upon their learned exercise
Never knew, could never tell
What their wisdom was about,
What their carnival was like,
Being in, being in, being always in
Where they never could get out
Of the everywhere, everything, always in,
To derive themselves from the Monoton.

SET III

Ding-Donging

With old hours all belfry heads
Are filled, as with thoughts.
With old hours ring the new hours
Between their bells.
And this hour-long ding-donging
So much employs the hour-long silences
That bells hang thinking when not striking,
When striking think of nothing.

Chimes of forgotten hours
More and more are played
While bells stare into space,
And more and more space wears
A look of having heard
But hearing not:
Forgotten hours chime louder
In the meantime, as if always,
And spread ding-donging back
More and more to yesterdays.

Because I Sit Here So

Because I sit here so,
Drooping and parched under this sun of sorrow,
I know
Somewhere
A flower or another like me
Hidden in a rare chance of difference
Wonders and withers unaccountably.

And if I sit here so,
Kindred and interlinked in circumstance
With others like me
Wherever I have been to dream —

And if I sit here so?

Stir me not,
Demons of the storm.
Were I as you would have me,
Astart with anger,
Gnawing the self-fold chain
Until the spell of unity break,
Madness would but thunder
Where sorrow had once burned,
A sun to smile in
And sit waiting under.

Because I sit here so,
Initiating in unrebellion
The perpetual ring
Of who are like me,
Death laughs along with us
And wears this garland of
Another and another and another
Dying alone, alike, unreasonably.

Faith upon the Waters

A ghost rose when the waves rose,
When the waves sank stood columnwise
And broken: archaic is
The spirituality of sea,
Water haunted by an imagination
Like fire previously.

More ghost when no ghost,
When the waves explain
Eye to the eye . . .

And dolphins tease,
And the ventriloquist gulls,
Their angular three-element cries . . .

Fancy ages.
A death-bed restlessness inflames the mind
And a warm mist attacks the face
With mortal premonition.

Beyond

Pain is impossible to describe
Pain is the impossibility of describing
Describing what is impossible to describe
Which must be a thing beyond description
Beyond description not to be known
Beyond knowing but not mystery
Not mystery but pain not plain but pain
But pain beyond but here beyond

O Vocables of Love

O vocables of love,
O zones of dreamt responses
Where wing on wing folds in
The negro centuries of sleep
And the thick lips compress
Compendiums of silence —

Throats claw the mirror of blind triumph,
Eyes pursue sight into the heart of terror.
Call within call
Succumbs to the indistinguishable
Wall within wall
Embracing the last crushed vocable,
The spoken unity of efforts.

O vocables of love,
The end of an end is an echo,
A last cry follows a last cry.
Finality of finality
Is perfection's touch of folly.
Ruin unfolds from ruin.
A remnant breeds a universe of fragment.
Horizons spread intelligibility
And once more it is yesterday.

Death as Death

To conceive death as death
Is difficulty come by easily,
A blankness fallen among
Images of understanding,
Death like a quick cold hand
On the hot slow head of suicide.
So is it come by easily
For one instant. Then again furnaces

Roar in the ears, then again hell revolves,
And the elastic eye holds paradise
At visible length from blindness,
And dazedly the body echoes
'Like this, like this, like nothing else.'

Like nothing — a similarity
Without resemblance. The prophetic eye,
Closing upon difficulty,
Opens upon comparison,
Halving the actuality
As a gift too plain, for which
Gratitude has no language,
Foresight no vision.

And I

And I,
And do I ask,
How long this pain?
Do I not show myself in every way
To be happy in what most ravages?

When I have grown old in these delights,
Then usedness and not exclaiming
May well seem unenthusiasm.

But now, in what am I remiss?
Wherein do I prefer
The better to the worse?

I will tell you.
There is a passing fault in her:
To be mild in my very fury.
And 'Beloved' she is called,
And pain I hunt alone

While she hangs back to smile,
Letting flattery crowd her round—
As if I hunted insult not true love.

But how may I be hated
Unto true love's all of me?
I will tell you.
The fury will grow into calm
As I grow into her
And, smiling always,
She looks serenely on their death-struggle,
Having looked serenely on mine.

Opening of Eyes

Thought looking out on thought
Makes one an eye.
One is the mind self-blind,
The other is thought gone
To be seen from afar and not known.
Thus is a universe very soon.

The immense surmise swims round and round,
And heads grow wise
Of marking bigness,
And idiot size
Spaces out Nature,

And ears report echoes first,
Then sounds, distinguish words
Of which the sense comes last —
From mouths spring forth vocabularies
As if by charm.
And thus do false horizons claim pride
For distance in the head
The head conceives outside.

Self-wonder, rushing from the eyes,
Returns lesson by lesson.
The all, secret at first,
Now is the knowable,
The view of flesh, mind's muchness.

But what of secretness,
Thought not divided, thinking
A single whole of seeing?
That mind dies ever instantly
Of too plain sight foreseen
Within too suddenly,
While mouthless lips break open
Mutely astonished to rehearse
The unutterable simple verse.

All Nothing, Nothing

The standing-stillness,
The from foot-to-foot,
Is no real illness,
Is no true fever,
Is no deep shiver;
The slow impatience
Is no sly conscience;
The covered cough bodes nothing,
Nor the covered laugh,
Nor the eye-to-eye shifting
Of the foot-to-foot lifting,
Nor the hands under-over,
Nor the neck and the waist
Twisting loose and then tight,
Right, left and right,
Nor the mind up and down
The long body column
With a know-not-why passion

And a can't-stop motion:
All nothing, nothing.

More death and discomfort
Were it
To walk away.
To fret and fidget
Is the ordinary.
To writhe and wriggle
Is the usual;
To walk away
Were a disgrace,
Were cowardice,
Were malice,
Would leave a mark and space
And were unbeautiful
And vain, oh, it were vain,
For none may walk away —
Who go, they stay,
And this is plain
In being general.

What, is their suspense
Clownish pretence?
What, are their grimaces
Silly-faces
And love of ghastliness?
What, is their anxiety and want
Teasing and taunt?
This scarcely,
This were a troublesome
Hypocrisy.

No, the twisting does not turn,
The stamping does not steam,
Nor the impatience burn,
Nor the tossing hearts scream,
Nor the bones fall apart

By the tossing of the heart,
Nor the heads roll off
With laugh-cough, laugh-cough,
Nor the backs crack with terror,
Nor the faces make martyr,
Nor love loathe
Nor loathing fondle
Nor pain rebel
Nor pride quarrel
Nor anything stir
In this stirring and standstill
Which is not natural,
Which is not trivial,
Not peaceful, not beautiful,
Altogether unwoeful,
Without significance
Or indeed further sense
Than going and returning
Within one inch,
Than rising and falling
Within one breath,
Than sweltering and shivering
Between one minute and the next
In the most artless
And least purposeful
Possibly purpose.

Grace

This posture and this manner suit
Not that I have an ease in them
But that I have a horror
And so stand well upright —
Lest, should I sit and, flesh-conversing, eat,
I choke upon a piece of my own tongue-meat.

The World and I

This is not exactly what I mean
Any more than the sun is the sun.
But how to mean more closely
If the sun shines but approximately?
What a world of awkwardness!
What hostile implements of sense!
Perhaps this is as close a meaning
As perhaps becomes such knowing.
Else I think the world and I
Must live together as strangers and die —
A sour love, each doubtful whether
Was ever a thing to love the other.
No, better for both to be nearly sure
Each of each — exactly where
Exactly I and exactly the world
Fail to meet by a moment, and a word.

Jewels and After

On the precious verge of danger
Jewels spring up to show the way,
The bejewelled way of danger,
Beautied with inevitability.

After danger the look-back reveals
Jewels only, dangerlessness,
Logic serened, unharshed into
A jewelled and loving progress.

And after danger's goal, what jewels?
Then none except death's plainest,
The unprecious jewels of safety,
As of childhood.

Footfalling

A modulation is that footfalling.
It says and does not say.
When not walking it is not saying.
When saying it is not walking.
When walking it is not saying.
Between the step and alternation
Breathes the hush of modulation
Which tars all roads
To confiding heels and soles and tiptoes.
Deep from the rostrum of the promenade
The echo-tongued mouth of motion
Rolls its voice,
And the large throat is heard to tremble
While the footfalls shuffle.

It says and does not say.
When the going is gone
There is only fancy.
Every thought sounds like a footfall,
Till a thought like a boot kicks down the wall.

Autobiography of the Present

Whole is by breaking and by mending.
The body is a day of ruin,
The mind, a moment of repair.
A day is not a day of mind
Until all lifetime is repaired despair.

To break, to day-long die,
To be not yet nor yet
Until dreaming is of having been,
Until dreaming is of having dreamed —

How in those days — how fast —
How fast we seemed to dream —
How fast we talked — how lost —
How lost the words until —
Until the pen ran down
To this awakened not forgetting.

But in those days always
How forgotten — and to say over —
To say now and now —
Or in a letter to say over soon —

Do you remember now, John,
Our suburban conversation once of bees?
Neatly at breakfast we of bees,
A retired talk or walk
Among the outskirts of profundity?
Slowly of honeycombs and swarms
And angry queens we?

But slowly bees is briefest dozing.
Between the country and the city,
Between sound sleep and walking,
More gives to pause and buzz than bees
A book about — and by —
Nor need tastes differ but to pause.

Do you remember now, John,
Do you remember my friend John
Who had a lordly not-to-hurry eye,
A very previous eye
In an advanced socket?

Yes, I remember.
And I remember my friend Norman,
Though by frugality of will
He shall arrive punctually to-morrow
When even the cinematograph of time

Has ceased to advertise to-day —
Though I remember.

Yes, she remembers all that seemed,
All that was like enough to now
To make a then as actual as then,
To make a now that succeeds only
By a more close resemblance to itself.

From *Come, Words, Away*

Come, words, away from mouths,
Away from tongues in mouths
And reckless hearts in tongues
And mouths in cautious heads —

Come, words, away to where
The meaning is not thickened
With the voice's fretting substance,
Nor look of words is curious
As letters in books staring out
All that man ever thought strange
And laid to sleep on white
Like the archaic manuscript
Of dreams at morning blacked on wonder.

Come, words, away to miracle
More natural than written art.
You are surely somewhat devils,
But I know a way to soothe
The whirl of you when speech blasphemes
Against the silent half of language
And, labouring the blab of mouths,
You tempt prolixity to ruin.
It is to fly you home from where
Like stealthy angels you made off once

On errands of uncertain mercy . . .
I know a way, unwild we'll mercy
And spread the largest news
Where never a folded ear dare make
A deaf division of entirety.

*   *   *

Not out of stranger-mouths then
Shall words unwind but from the voice
That haunted there like dumb ghost haunting
Birth prematurely, anxious of death.
Not ours those mouths long-lipped
To falsity and repetition
Whose frenzy you mistook
For loyal prophetic heat
To be improved but in precision.

*   *   *

Come, words, away,
And tell with me a story here,
Forgetting what's been said already:
That hell of hasty mouths removes
Into a cancelled heaven of mercies
By flight of words back to this plan
Whose grace goes out in utmost rings
To bounds of utmost storyhood.

SET IV

World's End

The tympanum is worn thin.
The iris is become transparent.
The sense has overlasted.
Sense itself is transparent.

Speed has caught up with speed.
Earth rounds out earth.
The mind puts the mind by.
Clear spectacle: where is the eye?

All is lost, no danger
Forces the heroic hand.
No bodies in bodies stand
Oppositely. The complete world
Is likeness in every corner.
The names of contrast fall
Into the widening centre.
A dry sea extends the universal.

No suit and no denial
Disturb the general proof.
Logic has logic, they remain
Locked in each other's arms,
Or were otherwise insane,
With all lost and nothing to prove
That even nothing can live through love.

The Flowering Urn

And every prodigal greatness
Must creep back into strange home,
Must fill the hollow matrix of
The never-begotten perfect son
Who never can be born.

And every quavering littleness
Must shrink more tinily than it knows
Into the giant hush whose sound
Reverberates within itself
As tenderest numbers cannot improve.

And from this jealous secrecy
Will rise the secret, will flower up
The likeness kept against false seed:
When death-whole is the seed
And no new harvest to fraction sowing.

Will rise the same peace that held
Before fertility's lie awoke
The virgin sleep of Mother All:
The same but for the way in flowering
It speaks of fruits that could not be.

Cure of Ignorance

The dogs still bark,
And something is not clear.
From ignorance dogs barked always.

How to enlighten them?
There are no dogs now —
They do but bark.

What is not clear is what is clear.
Dogs have the scent,
Yet nothing runs like prey.

Shall we seem to disappear
Until the dogs stop barking?
There is no other way to explain.

The Reasons of Each

The reason of the saint that he is saintly,
And of the hero that to him
Glory the mirror and the beauty;
And of the brigand that to prowl abhorred
Makes him renowned unto himself
And dear the evil name;

Of girls like evening angels
From the mass of heaven fluttering
To earth in wanton whispers —
That they invite their flesh to loose
All yet unbaptized terrors on them
And will to-morrow change the virgin glance
For the long wandering gaze;

The reason of the dark one that his heart
For love of hell is empty
And that the empty maze consoles
In that the bare heart is
Of heaven the augury
As of hell;

The reasons of each are lone,
And lone the fate of each.
To private death-ear will they tell
Why they have done so.
Such were the reasons of the lives they lived.
Then they are dead,
And the cause was themselves.

Each to himself is the cause of himself.
These are the agencies of freedom
Which necessity compels,
As birds are flown from earth
By that earth utters no command

Of fixity, but waits on motion
To consume itself, and stillness
To be earth of earth, ingenerate
Cohesion without cause.

For they are uncaused, the minds
Which differ not in sense.
They are the mind which saves
Sense to itself
Against interpretation's waste;
They are the sense dispartable
Which senses cannot change.

The reasons, then, of this one, that one,
That they unlike are this one, that one —
This is as the telling of beads.
The chain hangs round the neck of lamentation —
They are lost.
Or as to watch the sun's purposeful clouds
Mingle with moonlight and be nothing.

The brow of unanimity
Perplexes as each goes his unlike way.
But soon the vagrant thought is out of sight.
To go is short,
Though slow the shadow trailing after
Which the backward look a reason names.

That Ancient Line

Old Mother Act and her child Fact-of-Act
Lived practically as one,
He so proud of his monomaniac mother,
She so proud of her parthenogenetic son.

After her death he of course
With his looks and education
Lived on the formal compliments
That other phrases paid him;
And had, of his economy, one daughter
Who remarkably resembled
Her paternal and only grandmother.

Indeed, between Act and Matter-of-Fact
Was such consanguineous sympathy
That the disappearance of the matronymic
In the third generation of pure logic
Did not detract from the authority
Of this and later versions
Of the original progenitive argument.

Long flourished that estate
And never died that self-engendering line out.
Scion followed after scion
Until that ancient blood ran nearly thin.
But Verily, In Truth and Beyond Doubt
Renewed the inheritance — and And So On.

The Wind, The Clock, The We

The wind has at last got into the clock —
Every minute for itself.
There's no more sixty,
There's no more twelve,
It's as late as it's early.

The rain has washed out the numbers.
The trees don't care what happens.
Time has become a landscape
Of suicidal leaves and stoic branches —
Unpainted as fast as painted.

65

Or perhaps that's too much to say,
With the clock devouring itself
And the minutes given leave to die.

The sea's no picture at all.
To sea, then: that's time now,
And every mortal heart's a sailor
Sworn to vengeance on the wind,
To hurl life back into the thin teeth
Out of which first it whistled,
An idiotic defiance of it knew not what
Screeching round the studying clock.

Now there's neither ticking nor blowing.
The ship has gone down with its men,
The sea with the ship, the wind with the sea.
The wind at last got into the clock,
The clock at last got into the wind,
The world at last got out of itself.

At last we can make sense, you and I,
You lone survivors on paper,
The wind's boldness and the clock's care
Become a voiceless language,
And I the story hushed in it —
Is more to say of me?
Do I say more than self-choked falsity
Can repeat word for word after me,
The script not altered by a breath
Of perhaps meaning otherwise?

Poet: A Lying Word

You have now come with me, I have now come with you, to the
season that should be winter, and is not: we have not come back.

66

We have not come back: we have not come round: we have not moved. I have taken you, you have taken me, to the next and next span, and the last — and it is the last. Stand against me then and stare well through me then. It is a wall not to be scaled and left behind like the old seasons, like the poets who were the seasons.

Stand against me then and stare well through me then. I am no poet as you have span by span leapt the high words to the next depth and season, the next season always, the last always, and the next. I am a true wall: you may but stare me through.

It is a false wall, a poet: it is a lying word. It is a wall that closes and does not.

This is no wall that closes and does not. It is a wall to see into, it is no other season's height. Beyond it lies no depth and height of further travel, no partial courses. Stand against me then and stare well through me then. Like wall of poet here I rise, but am no poet as walls have risen between next and next and made false end to leap. A last, true wall am I: you may but stare me through.

And the tale is no more of the going: no more a poet's tale of a going false-like to a seeing. The tale is of a seeing true-like to a knowing: there's but to stare the wall through now, well through.

It is not a wall, it is not a poet. It is not a lying wall, it is not a lying word. It is a written edge of time. Step not across, for then into my mouth, my eyes, you fall. Come close, stare me well through, speak as you see. But, oh, infatuated drove of lives, step not across now. Into my mouth, my eyes, shall you thus fall, and be yourselves no more.

Into my mouth, my eyes, I say, I say. I am no poet like transitory wall to lead you on into such slow terrain of time as measured out your single span to broken turns of season once and once again.

67

I lead you not. You have now come with me, I have now come with you, to your last turn and season: thus could I come with you, thus only.

I say, I say, I am, it is, such wall, such poet, such not lying, such not leading into. Await the sight, and look well through, know by such standing still that next comes none of you.

Comes what? Comes this even I, even this not-I, this not lying season when death holds the year at steady count — this every-year.

Would you not see, not know, not mark the count? What would you then? Why have you come here then? To leap a wall that is no wall, and a true wall? To step across into my eyes and mouth not yours? To cry me down like wall or poet as often your way led past down-falling height that seemed?

I say, I say, I am, it is: such wall, such end of graded travel. And if you will not hark, come tumbling then upon me, into my eyes, my mouth, and be the backward utterance of yourselves expiring angrily through instant seasons that played you time-false.

My eyes, my mouth, my hovering hands, my intransmutable head: wherein my eyes, my mouth, my hands, my head, my body-self, are not such mortal simulacrum as everlong you builded against very-death, to keep you everlong in boasted death-course, neverlong? I say, I say, I am not builded of you so.

This body-self, this wall, this poet-like address, is that last barrier long shied of in your elliptic changes: out of your leaping, shying, season-quibbling, have I made it, is it made. And if now poet-like it rings with one-more-time as if, this is the mounted stupor of your everlong outbiding worn prompt and lyric, poet-like — the forbidden one-more-time worn time-like.

Does it seem I ring, I sing, I rhyme, I poet-wit? Shame on me then! Grin me your foulest humour then of poet-piety, your eyes

68

rolled up in white hypocrisy — should I be one sprite more of your versed fame — or turned from me into your historied brain, where the lines read more actual. Shame on me then!

And haste unto us both, my shame is yours. How long I seem to beckon like a wall beyond which stretches longer length of flesh-some traverse: it is your lie of flesh and my flesh-seeming stand of words. Haste then unto us both. I say, I say. This wall reads 'Stop!' This poet verses 'Poet: a lying word!'

Shall the wall then not crumble, as to walls is given? Have I not said: 'Stare me well through'? It is indeed a wall, crumble it shall. It is a wall of walls, stare it well through: the reading gentles near, the name of death passes with the season that it was not.

Death is a very wall. The going over walls, against walls, is a dying and a learning. Death is a knowing-death. Known death is truth sighted at the halt. The name of death passes. The mouth that moves with death forgets the word.

And the first page is the last of death. And haste unto us both, lest the wall seem to crumble not, to lead mock-onward. And the first page reads: 'Haste unto us both!' And the first page reads: 'Slowly, it is the first page only.'

Slowly, it is the page before the first page only, there is no haste. The page before the first page tells of death, haste, slowness: how truth falls true now at the turn of page, at time of telling. Truth one by one falls true. And the first page reads, the page which is the page before the first page only: 'This once-upon-a-time when seasons failed, and time stared through the wall nor made to leap across, is the hour, the season, seasons, year and years, no wall and wall, where when and when the classic lie dissolves and nakedly time salted is with truth's sweet flood nor yet to mix with, but be salted tidal-sweet — O sacramental ultimate by which shall time be old-renewed nor yet another season move.' I say, I say.

With the Face

With the face goes a mirror
As with the mind a world.
Likeness tells the doubting eye
That strangeness is not strange.
At an early hour and knowledge
Identity not yet familiar
Looks back upon itself from later,
And seems itself.

To-day seems now.
With reality-to-be goes time.
With the mind goes a world.
With the heart goes a weather.
With the face goes a mirror
As with the body a fear.
Young self goes staring to the wall
Where dumb futurity speaks calm,
And between then and then
Forebeing grows of age.

The mirror mixes with the eye.
Soon will it be the very eye.
Soon will the eye that was
The very mirror be.
Death, the final image, will shine
Transparently not otherwise
Than as the dark sun described
With such faint brightnesses.

The Time Beneath

In the premortuary tomb
Of ancient time —
Who does not lie there,
A mummy not yet born?
Who does not lie there,
Who lives?
Except mock-creatures in wild numbers
The upper air usurping
While the great dead still sleep?

But when the great dead at last live,
What are those deep worlds then?
When beauty rises from the blackened queens
And the lachrymatory vessels sparkle
With tears from unbound eyes
That grieve sincerely how they lay
Long closed?

They are the pit of future then,
Where cautious souls that never risked name
Lie down in ghastly triumph of will
And dream of grandeur never lost
To the ancient test of death.

I Am

I am an indicated other:
Witness this common presence
Intelligible to the common mind,
The daylight census.

I am a such-and-such appearance
Listed among the furnitures

Of the proprietary epoch
That on the tattered throne of time
Effects inheritance still,
Though of shadow that estate now,
Death-dim, memory illumined.

You, spent kingdom of the senses,
Have laid hands on the unseeable,
Shadow's seeming fellow:
And all together we
A population of names only
Inhabiting the hypothetic streets,
Where no one can be found
Ever at home.

Where then, fellow-citizens
Of this post-carnal matter,
Is each the next and next one,
Stretching the instant chain
Toward its first-last link,
The twilight that into dawn passes
Without intervention of night,
Time's slow terrible enemy?

That I with you did lie
In the same love-bed, same planet
Of thinking bright against
The black pervasion, against the sleep
That gives not back if none makes argument
That yesterday is self still —

That I thus to you am like,
That I walk beside and straight
On your same circle of argument,
That I walked, that I was,
That I slept, that I lived —

That I live — let me be a proof
Of a world as was a world,
And accept it, King Habit,
From my mouth, our mouth.

But where, where?
If I have so companioned?
Here, here!

The same not-here I ever held,
And be it yours, and I yours,
Out of my mouth until
You tire of the possession
And, falling prone, relinquish
The stale breath of stubbornness.

Then will this still be here,
Here, here, the proved not-here
Of perfect contradiction —
Here where you visited on me
The individual genius, paradox.

And I will then stand you up,
To count you mine, since dying frenzy
Makes new dwelling-charm,
O entranced wizards of place-magic.
I, in the over-reaching moment,
In the reign one-too-many,
Dynasty too-long of time-kind —
I, created time-kind by commingling
Of the jealous substance with
The different way to be —

I, out of your stopped mouth, our mouth,
Will spin round continuity,
Winding the thread me round
To keep these other years safe
Always and always while you haunt

The windows that might be here,
Looking for sign of elsewhere —
If I perhaps such same fatality
As before fast was magicked
Into the this-year dialects.

Divestment of Beauty

She, she and she and she —
Which of these is not lovely?
In her long robe of glamour now
And her beauty like a ribbon tied
The wisdom of her head round?

To call these 'women'
Is homage of the eye:
Such sights to greet as natural,
Such beings to proclaim
Companion to expectance.

But were they now who take
This gaudy franchise from
The accolade of stilted vision
Their lady-swaddlings to unwrap
And shed the timorous scales of nakedness —

It were a loathsome spectacle, you think?
Eventual entrails of deity
Worshipful eye offending?
It were the sign, man,
To pluck the loathsome eye,

Forswear the imbecile
Theology of loveliness,
Be no more doctor in antiquities —
Chimeras of the future
In archaic daze embalmed —

And grow to later youth,
Felling the patriarchal leer
That it lie reft of all obscentities
While she and she, she, she, disclose
The recondite familiar to your candour.

From *Three Sermons to the Dead*

The Way of the Air

The way of the air is by clouds to speak
And by clouds to be silent.
The way of the air is a progress
From treachery to repentance.
The air is the freedom to hope.
You breathe your hopes,
And are glad, and live.
And there are clouds.
There are clouds which betray your hopes.
To whom? To your Conscience, which is not you.
And you are ashamed, and the clouds tear.
By the conscienceless air you live,
But by Conscience, your mouth's tight seal,
You die, you are what you are only.
The clouds are you, Conscience is not you.
Yet you make the clouds to tear and repent
For Conscience's sake, which is not you.
For first was the air, and last is Conscience.
And that which is last is, and that which was first is not.
First was freedom, and last is a tight seal.
The free word tears, but the sealed mouth is silenter.
The air opens your mouth, the clouds unshape it.
Conscience closes the mouth, but gives it back.
What is Conscience? It is Death —
In airless final love of which
You keep inviolate your voice

Against the clouds that steam in traitor whispers
Repentantly upon your mouth,
Aura of tattered hopes
Protesting as you dare not.

Auspice of Jewels

They have connived at those jewelled fascinations
That to our hands and arms and ears
And heads and necks and feet
And all the winding stalk
Extended the mute spell of the face.

They have endowed the whole of us
With such a solemn gleaming
As in the dark of flesh-love
But the face at first did have.
We are studded with wide brilliance
As the world with towns and cities —
The travelling look builds capitals
Where the evasive eye may rest
Safe from the too immediate lodgement.

Obscure and bright these forms
Which as the women of their lingering thought
In slow translucence we have worn.
And the silent given glitter locks us
In a not false unplainness:
Have we ourselves been sure
What steady countenance to turn them?

Until now — when this passionate neglect
Of theirs, and our twinkling reluctance,
Are like the reader and the book
Whose fingers and whose pages have confided
But whose sight and sense
Meet in a chilly time of strangeness;

And it is once more early, anxious,
And so late, it is intolerably the same
Not speaking coruscation
That both we and they made endless, dream-long,
Lest be cruel to so much love
The closer shine of waking,
And what be said sound colder
Than the ghastly love-lisp.

Until now — when to go jewelled
We must despoil the drowsy masquerade
Where gloom of silk and gold
And glossy dazed adornments
Kept safe from flagrant realness
The forgeries of ourselves we were —
When to be alive as love feigned us
We must steal death and its wan splendours
From the women of their sighs we were.

For we are now otherwise luminous.
The light which was spent in jewels
Has performed upon the face
A gradual eclipse of recognition.
We have passed from plaintive visibility
Into total rareness,
And from this reunion of ourselves and them
Under the snuffed lantern of time
Comes an astonished flash like truth
Or the unseen-unheard entrance of someone
Whom eyes and ears in their dotage
Have forgotten for dead or lost.

(And hurrying towards distracted glory,
Gemmed lady-pageants, bells on their hearts,
By restless knights attended
Whose maudlin plumes and pommels
Urge the adventure past return.)

On a New Generation

What may be born of the anxious union
Between perplexed man and irresolute woman
Is only, by this fertile speculation,
The either animal whose destiny
Differs from hers or his
By only the so many forepledged years
Of advance in irresolution or perplexity.

Yet the new girl more shines with herself,
And the latest boy has a light in his head.
Not unlikely they will speak to each other
In a peculiar way and forget nature,
Then to fall quiet like a house no more haunted.
And in such silence may enough centuries fade
For all the loud births to be eloquently unmade.

Tree-Sense

Numbers in heaven grow
As trees constrained between
Air and tight soil resolve
Divided heart by dancing
To the supposed music of earth
But with thoughts birdwise away —
Imagining and motionless.
In heaven are such parliaments
Opinionating of eternity;
Other the forestry of hell
Where rugged communities of will,
In tawdry treedom spread as cities,
Their foliate hates make boundless night of.

But how — to instruct of heaven
And to use hell's name for hell,
And the time surely far off yet
To speak identical, word same as sense?
What is God and what the devil
If tree-metaphors suffice
To tell immediately of?
God is pale doubt, the devil bright denial.
Heaven perhaps next year, hell the last,
And the multitudes prophetic remnants
Of the millennial no-one.

And the time far off yet?
By less than any minute more,
By the slight scratching of the pen —
And to read the written story over,
Eyes still from trees green-fresh
And full of tangled nature
Still wondering which thing to be,
What's most and best and fruitfullest
When drops the lightning season
And all together's added up.

And will the sum be ever spelt
In other science than such numbers
Forward and backward bargaining
The errors with the answer?
The trees this year grow wide and tall,
The sun stands off great to watch,
And surely there's a world abroad
To which the world-end calling
Is a mere unseen humming, a voice
In the slow branches muffled,
Musing how long yet is to be not loud,
To be a breath outside time's lungs —
Uncalendared soft truth still.

But surely truth is very old,
Very old, all but learnt, all but taught?
Does myself confound, that I speak?
Do yourselves hinder, that you hear?
That in tree-grammar we converse,
Since trees beside myself and you are?
Shall we then put away the book
And you and me and close the schoolroom?
But the trees that this year a year
May still be languaging as if
The time were still far off yet?

The trees will come along, as fast
As slow as you came, coming
The pace it pleased you —
As the trees please, and you . . .

Else the time's gone like time
For walking out of time and into
Not-time, passing the trees by —
The trees, the present pleasantness
Of future future yet,
Not now or now, while life now lives,
Now lives, now lived — oh, coloured twilight,
Nearly immortal death.

From *Disclaimer of Person*

Suspicion like the earth is hard
And like the earth opposes
Dense fact to the doubtable:
Which therefore like the air surrenders
Semblance to the bolder sights.
I have surrendered place
To many solid miles of brain-rote,
To the just so many matters and no more
That reason, grudging prodigal,

Allows numerous, consecutive.
Even in my own mind I have stood last,
An airy exile, nothing, nowhere,
My eyes obeying laws of circumspection
By which myself shone fanciful
In lurid never:
Because that had been so, I not.
But as time learns a boredom,
Loathes the determinate succession,
Irks with uncalendared event
And brings surprise to be,
The natural conscience snapped in me —
And lo! I was, I am.
Elastic logic thinning
Grows delicate to marvels.
Fine argument at finest disembroils
The ravelled choking maze of caution.
The sudden of the slow is bred,
The curious of the common.
Into the sceptic fog that mists
Infraction from the chronic rule
Stumbles intelligence a-rage
To find the unthought wanton thought
And, self-confounding, think it.
My life, with other lives a world,
With other ways of being a coiled nature,
Springs separate: I am personified,
Of being caught in that pressed confluence
And proven look-substantial,
Yet strange to the familiar soul
In fellowed course entwined.
Acquaintance marks out unacquaintance.
Usage has bound of mystery.
The continents of vision view
A further which grows spatial
From lying next, in dark increase
Of the gregarious light with which
Compacting sense embraces straggling all.

*   *   *

. . . So have I lived,
Approaching rhythms of old circumstance
To the perilous margin, moment.
And struck the string which breaks at sounding,
Taken the tremorless note to mouth,
And spoken sound's inversion
Like a statue moved with stillness.
This is that latest all-risk:
An I which mine is for the courage
No other to be, if not danger's self.
Nor did I other become, others,
In braving all-risk with hushed step,
Mind rattling veteran armouries.

*   *   *

If this be I.
If words from earthy durance loosed
To earthy right of meaning
Cannot belie their wisdoming,
The doubt-schooled care that bent back sense
From skyish startle, faith's delirium.
If I my words am,
If the footed head which frowns them
And the handed heart which smiles them
Are the very writing, table, chair,
The paper, pen, self, taut community
Wherein enigma's orb is word-constrained.
Does myself upon the page meet,
Does the thronging firm a name
To nod my own—witnessing
I write or am this, it is written?
What thinks the world?
Has here the time-eclipsed occasion
Grown language-present?
Or does the world demand,
And what think I?
The world in me which fleet to disavow

Ordains perpetual reiteration?
And these the words ensuing.

Doom in Bloom

Now flower the oldest seeds.
The secret of the root no more
Keeps jealous distance from the air.
The dark intent, so lothfully ascending,
At last to resolution grows;
The glance of long reluctance shows.

Weakly we write upon
The closing surface of oblivion.
Our faith in earth, in nether sameness,
Hurries to take the separate colour.
And leaning on the faded air
We flaunt ourselves against despair.

Gruesomely joined in hate
Of unlike efflorescence,
We were a cruel compacted silence
From which unlovable centuries sprang.
But time has knit so hard a crust
That speak and differ now we must —

Or be in pride encased
Until the living way has ceased
And only death comes to occur.
Though half our zeal but fair is,
Spells but an earth's variety,
Hope makes a stronger half to beauty
When from the deep bed torn
Of ultimate misgiving

An auspice of like peril to bring.
The lone defiance blossoms failure,
But risk of all by all beguiles
Fate's wreckage into similar smiles.

From *Benedictory*

. . . .

The mystery wherein we
Accustomed grew as to the dark
Has now been seen enough —
I have seen, you have seen.

*　*　*

It seems not now distressful
Or yet too much delighted in.
It was a mystery endured
Until a fuller sense befall.

*　*　*

The fuller sense and cause became
That old and older mystery
As you more unremembered
That oldest sense you never knew.

*　*　*

We have now seen, already seen,
Through folded clouds and folded meaning
The blindness and the evilness
That so have we been wrapped.

*　*　*

You have pretended to be seeing.
I have pretended that you saw.
So came we by such eyes —
And within mystery to have language.

The cause was that a way lacked.
It seemed a wayless world like no world.
You made a way and a world
Which no way was, nor any world.

*   *   *

There was no sight to see.
That which is to be seen is no sight.
You made it a sight to see.
It is no sight, and this was the cause.

Now, having seen, let our eyes close
And a dark blessing pass among us —
A quick-slow blessing to have seen
And said and done no worse or better.

And slowly wait — slowly it happened
A way and a world to be made,
And to seem the way and the world
Which must be so if aught is.

*   *   *

We shall be wholly joined.
We were then but a patched crowd.
We stood outside us then
Like friendship in vague streets.

And I stood with you,
Against that, soon or sooner,
A blessing and a parting must
Send home from home.

Against this parting so to meet
I stood with you, and did, and said.
Here wholly shall we love and meet
And be not, and I least.

85

A blessing on us all, on our last folly,
That we part and give blessing.
Yet a folly to be done
A greater one to spare.

*   *   *

For in no wise shall it be
As it is, as it has been.
A blessing on us all,
That we shall in no wise be as we were.
. . . .

After So Much Loss

After so much loss —
Seeming of gain,
Seeming of loss —
Subsides the swell of indignation
To the usual rhythm of the year.

The coward primroses are up,
We contract their profuse mildness.
Women with yet a few springs to live
Clutch them in suppliant bouquets
On the way to relatives,
Who, no, do not begrudge
This postponement of funerals.
And, oh, how never tired, and tired,
The world of primroses, how spring
The bended spirit fascinates
With promise of revival,
Leaving more honest summer to proclaim
That this is all — a brighter disappointment —
Time has to give to an implacable
Persuasion of things lost, wrongly.

Is it to wonder, then,
That we defy the unsuspecting moment,
Release our legs from the year's music,
And, to the reckless strum of hate,
Dance — grinding from primroses the tears
They never of themselves would have shed?
None dances whom no hate stirs,
Who has not lost and loathed the loss,
Who does not feel deprived.
Slyest rebellion of the feet,
The chaste and tremulous disport
Of children, limbs in passionless wave —
None dances whom no hate stirs,
Or shall not stir.

As sure as primrosed spring betides,
After so much loss,
The hate will out, the dance be on,
And many of their rage fall down.
It is easy as spring to yield to the year,
And easy as dance to break with the year.
But to go with the year in partition
Between seeming loss, seeming gain,
That is the difficult decorum.
Nor are the primroses unwelcome.

From *The Last Covenant*

If ever had a covenant been sought,
If ever truth had been like night sat up with
As one house in a city may till dawn
With sleepless lamp eke out the day before —

But the war that was, and again was,
Never did it lapse, never was there peace,
A vigil sworn to peace, peace only.

Never was there not, in hearts, on tongues,
A protest of to-morrows,
According to the desire of the heart,
And to the will of the tongue.

There were never covenants:
The covenants which are told of were but trials.
There have been trials but never covenants.
Man is a fretful man, truth is a patient goal,
An end which waits all ending.
Between fretfulness and patience have been trials.
Races have been run and won,
Triumphs foretold, and triumphs celebrated.
But never between man and truth
Has been less strife than a kiss's strife;
Never has man more than loved;
Never has he not, fretful, torn the embrace,
Never rested but he rose,
Never covenanted but he bargained.

*　　*　　*

There has been much mist always.
A day often is named fair.
But never clouds lack, though soft to see,
Where to-morrow's passions huddle,
And which to-morrow will make weather of,
Even the natural temper of a day.
Between death and death hovers the course of man.
Much mist attends his time,
Banks of obscurity ensphere his place.
His world has been a fitful veering,
Paling and blush of troth and impulse,
Pleasure and resolve.

He has scored shadowy vantages on air,
Mounted among the ruins of self
The weary trophies of intransigence.
These are not immortalities, nor monuments,

88

But rotting gages, limp where thrown,
Relics of dreamt victories.
For truth is no historian,
To touch the random scene
With probability's enchantment.

* * *

From where the power, so to continue
In more days, more semblances?
Is truth then to be parried
With the instruments of time,
Taunted with prematurities —
A future ever future?
Whose the power,
If man has power to proclaim,
'Here is state, and this the rule,'
And there take stand, and that make master?
It is a borrowed power,
If not returned is taken away;
And the end, death,
As in a foreign country,
Not as the fortunate bring travel home
To native recognition and embrace.

Roses are buds, and beautiful,
One petal leaning toward adventure.
Roses are full, all petals forward,
Beauty and power indistinguishable.
Roses are blown, startled with life,
Death young in their faces.
Shall they die?
Then comes the halt, and recumbence, and failing.
But none says, 'A rose is dead.'
But men die: it is said, it is seen.
For a man is a long, late adventure;
His budding is a purpose,
His fullness more purpose,

His blowing a renewal,
His death a cramped spilling
Of rash measures and miles.
To the roses no tears:
Which flee before the race is called.
And to man no mercy but his will:
That he has had his will, and is done.
The mercy of truth — it is to be truth.

*   *   *

There shall be a world,
And it shall be so, and its things so,
In being world entire,
Nor such seizure of truth, or such —
Time's empty grasp.
You shall have:
By that your having shows
Small in your hand,
And the hand known for small.
Thus is the sweet possession true,
And the holding of it good.
You shall have delight in these furnishings;
And it shall be well beyond delightful —
You shall know it to be well.
But what sights, tastes, sounds,
What feel and fragrance?

*   *   *

And must these be proved?
Ticketed with legends that they *are* so?

*   *   *

You shall leave those places,
Each a camp raised in a shifting wilderness;
And no camp stayed its wilderness,
But wandered with it, into failing distance.

You shall reach this place.
You shall prophesy: 'I have arrived here
And will discover to myself what *is* here.'

But not because of you,
That you shall have better, know better,
Than you had, than you knew,
Is truth that delight, that truth,
That lengthened age
Past death's abrupt meridian —
The temporal habit put away
Like drudging error.

*　　*　　*

Not because of you, not because of her,
That you had need, that she had need,
But that toward this far verge
The far surmises, ships of roving chance:
The way is over sullen depths,
Round angry headlands,
Listing past ghostly settlements
(Coasts of the dogged dead),
And nowhere making port.
The way is onward,
And travel has one end,
This unitary somewhere.

*　　*　　*

The Forgiven Past

That once which pained to think of,
Like a promise to oneself not kept
Nor keepable, now is grown mild.
The thistle-patch of memory
Claims our confiding touch;

The naked spurs do not draw blood,
Yielding to stoic pressure
With awkward flexibility.

We are glad it happened so
Which long seemed traitorous to hope,
False to the destined Otherwise;
Since by those failures-of-the-time
We learned the skill of failure, time —
Waiting to hold the seal of truth
With a less eager hand,
Sparing the authentic signature
For the most prudent sanctions,
Lest the wax and ink of faith be used
Before to hope's reverses
Succeed the just realities,
And we be spent of welcome
Save for a withered smile.

The transformation of old grief
Into a present grace of mind
Among the early shadows which
The present light inhabit,
As the portentous universe
Now upon earth descends
Timidly, in nostalgic bands
Of elemental trials and errors:
This is how truth is groved,
With wayside nights where sleeping
We wake to tell what once seemed cruel
As dream-dim — in the dream
As plain and sure as then,
In telling no less dark than doubtful.

This is how pleasure relives history,
Like accusation that at last
Settling unrancorous on lies
Gives kinder names to them —

When truth is so familiar
That the false no more than strange is,
Nor wondrous evil strange
But of a beggar's right to tenderness
Whom once in robes of certainty
We stood upon illusion's stage
And then, to expiate our self-deceit,
Sent forth in honesty's ill rags.

Nothing So Far

Nothing so far but moonlight
Where the mind is;
Nothing in that place, this hold,
To hold;
Only their faceless shadows to announce
Perhaps they come—
Nor even do they know
Whereto they cast them.

Yet here, all that remains
When each has been the universe:
No universe, but each, or nothing.
Here is the future swell curved round
To all that was.

What were we, then,
Before the being of ourselves began?
Nothing so far but strangeness
Where the moments of the mind return.
Nearly, the place was lost
In that we went to stranger places.

Nothing so far but nearly
The long familiar pang
Of never having gone;

And words below a whisper which
If tended as the graves of live men should be
May bring their names and faces home.

It makes a loving promise to itself,
Womanly, that there
More presences are promised
Than by the difficult light appear.
Nothing appears but moonlight's morning —
By which to count were as to strew
The look of day with last night's rid of moths.